© 2019 Laura Stroebel

AcuteByDesign Publishing

Softcover ISBN: 978-1-943515-07-3
Hardcover ISBN: 978-1-943515-09-7

All rights reserved including the right of reproduction in whole or in part in any form and in any language without written permission of AcuteByDesign, except for limited excerpts for the purpose of providing reviews.

AcuteByDesign
the little book company that could
A Michael Marion Sharpe Company

Animals Are People Too

Poems and Pictures by
Laura Stroebel

Acknowledgments

I would like to thank all the wonderful Connecticut farmers who allowed me to photograph their animals. I learned so much about your farms and how important it is to support our local businesses in this beautiful pastoral state.

Thank you to the Secchiaroli Piggery, Salem's Antique Carriage and Farm Museum, Foster Hill Farm, ME Llama Farm, Lindy Farms, Tiffany Farms, Dragon Fire Mousery, Stacy Jorgensen, and Lynn Chacho.

A special shout out to my family for believing in my pursuit of poetry and photography and of course we wouldn't be reading this right now if it weren't for the support and creativity of AcuteByDesign publisher Michael Marion Sharpe and editor Cynthia MacGregor. Thank you so much for making this happen!

Contents

1 – Cassandra the Cow
2 – Tough Kitty-Witty
3 – Howly McHowl
4 - Ms. Beautimus
5 – Famous Shamus
6 – Billy the Bully
7 – Ramone
8 – Elton
9 – Riddhi
10. – Malarkey Mouse
11 – Latisha Llama
12 – Dudley the Donkey

Introduction

These poems and pictures are for all the unique children in the world, all those quirky little habits and mannerisms we have that make us special and who we are. You may see yourself as really angry some days like Tough-Kitty Witty and want to take out your claws, or maybe you are more like Dudley the Donkey and don't always tell the truth, or maybe you are a mix.

What really matters is that we try to understand one another, that we take the time and make the effort to teach and learn from one another. With compassion and understanding, there is hope—that we can form new friendships and make a kinder world to live in. That is my dream, anyway.

~ L.S.

1. Cassandra the Cow

Cassandra the cow
Just didn't know how
To get along with her brothers.

She'd moo and she'd cry
And kick her hooves high.
She was seeking attention of others.

They'd all dash away.
In the field they would stay,
Afar from her baby-like squawking.

They'd look and they'd giggle,
Their tails they would wiggle,
They'd tease with their low-whispered talking.

So sad and alone,
In the field Cassie'd moan,
"Why don't all the other cows like me?"

Then a mouse near the wall
Stood up really tall,
And said, "Being yourself is the key!"

"Don't put on an act
To be part of a pack.
Be true to yourself, that is all."

"Don't cry for attention
Be kind, try to listen,
You'll find other cows will soon call."

Cassie hugged the kind mouse,
And went back to her house
And stopped making such an ol' ruckus.

She listened to questions
And offered suggestions.
Her friendships were now a success.

2. Tough Kitty-Witty

Tough Kitty-Witty would put up her mitties,
Ready to strike up a fight,
If someone would tend her, or tried to befriend her,
Sharp claws quickly turned them to flight.

Born in a gutter, curled under a shutter,
Kitty-Witty knew nothing of care.
She had to make do on garbage to chew,
No parent had ever been there.

One day a stray kitty slunk over to Witty,
With ribs poking out of its side.
The tiny thing mewed. Kitty-Witty thought, "Rude!"
And shoved the small baby aside.

He let out a yelp. He just needed help,
And thought that a friend would be swell.
When a tear landed near, Kitty-Witty saw fear,
And knew that emotion quite well.

Stray Kitty stayed longer, and Witty grew fonder.
The pals traveled thick as two thieves,
Now when Stray Kitty sees other kittens in need,
Witty says, "Let us do a good deed."

3. Howly McHowl

Howly McHowl
Did nothing but scowl
And sang a sad tune every night.

When his owners left home
He'd sit all alone
Making his vocals just right.

When his folks would come back,
They'd give him a pat,
Then ignore him until time for bed.

He would curl by the door
And cry all the more
'Til morning, and wait to be fed.

The neighbors, ticked off,
Would call, in tones rough,
"Please keep all that howling at bay."

The owners confessed
"We think he's depressed,"
But shrugged the dog's problem away.

A ten-year-old boy
Took out an old toy
And said, "I'll tend Howly for you!"

The crowd looked at him
And then on a whim
Thought, "Maybe this boy has a clue."

The two went away.
In the yard they would play,
Long hours and into the dark.

With love from the boy
McHowl has found joy.
He has no more reason to bark.

4. Ms. Beautimus

Ms. Beautimus, the speckled hen,
So lovely as a dream,
Would cluck her tune among the trees,
A feathered song supreme.

Her voice drew sunshine from above,
Skies cherished all the notes.
A rainbow showered o'er her nest
On air her music floats.

The other hens would try their best,
But no grand light would come,
No sunshine near, no rainbows dear.
The other birds were glum.

So one day all these jealous hens
Decided to be mean.
As Ms. B. slept, in nest they crept
And plucked her feathers clean.

Like ice she was within the night
And caught a nasty cold.
A cough was born upon her breast—
No voice was to be told.

Poor Beautimus could sing no more.
Heartbroken, she would cry,
So sad without her gift to give,
She lost her will to try.

The other birds were all confused.
They'd thought they would be pleased.
Without her song to start their day
Such sadness they were seized.

Their jealousy had hurt their friend
They knew that they'd been wrong.
Would she forgive their ugly deed?
They missed her sweet, warm song.

They clucked out an apology
They said they should know better.
No feathers, now, to keep her warm?
They knit Ms. B. a sweater.

In time her voice came back again
And, after that, her feathers.
The woods were filled with lovely song
Of friends who sang together.

5. Famous Shamus

**Famous Shamus was loved by all.
A good-looking sheep at four feet tall
With a gift of gab, he told his stories
Of times on the farm and ancient glories.**

**The animals crowded round him near
As his funny tales filled them with cheer.
At night's end when they would all retire,
The audience left, each to home fire.**

Shamus, they thought, had plenty of friends,
So they never invited him back to their pens.
Shamus would travel alone in the night,
Deep in thought and far out of sight.

He'd sit on his bed. He'd sigh, feeling glum.
"I've no one to talk to. I just need a chum.
I'm Famous Shamus, but famous for what?
If I had a friend, it would help a lot."

One night an old pig, named Smelly, in fact
Needed Shamus's help for his comedy act.
So he stayed out all night for Shamus's show
Then afterward said, "Now where should we go?"

Surprised, Shamus asked, "Going back to your pen?"
"Oh, I haven't had one since don't know when.
My friends say I'm funny, they like all my jokes,
But I need your advice, to write for my folks."

"Come over here, Smelly. Let's go to my barn.
I'd love to talk business and share an old yarn."
Smelly was happy, there was warmth and good food.
Shamus was smiling—Smelly brightened his mood.

The two got on smashing, as great as can be.
Smelly opened for Shamus, huge crowds they did see.
So a roommate he'd found. Shamus wasn't alone.
And Smelly, his sidekick, had found a new home.

6. Billy the Bully

The farmyard was gathered
With a problem that mattered:
How to deal with a mean, nasty goat

Who delighted in picking
On new kids by kicking
Them straight in the head or the throat.

Billy the Bully
Was dirty and woolly
With cuts to his face and his feet.

He'd show you his muscle
Then get in a tussle
And kick you clear into next week.

He cared not one oat
If you bit off his coat
Or screamed as you ran round the place.

He'd laugh all the more
While you cried on the floor,
Then tell you "Get out of my face."

But one day Old Billy
Met new goat, Sweet Lily,
Who shyly appeared at his side.

She rubbed on his coat
Like a kind, loving goat.
He froze in his steps. Eyes went wide.

She said, "My advice:
Is to start being nice.
I can't have you hurting my friends."

Now, make up your mind
To learn to be kind.
Our goat family needs this to end.

Billy the Bully
Was flustered and woolly
He mumbled he'd give it a go.

He'd never been gentle
Or even parental.
But slowly his kindness did grow.

Now in the goat pen
The babies love him,
Around him they caper and dance.

As Sweet Lilly guided
His anger subsided
The bully now has a new chance.

7. Ramone

Ramone was unique.
His coat shone in the sun.
For a horse he was sleek,
And oh boy could he run.

With speed he was gifted,
A joy to behold.
His hooves fully lifted—
His racing? Pure gold.

But he kept a secret
From all of the others
He had a small defect:
He couldn't see colors.

No bright sunny rainbows
Or fall sunrise haze,
No pretty green meadows—
Just visions of grays.

Then a race came to town.
Flags quickly were raised.
The first one came down.
Ramone looked around, dazed.

The horses were gated,
Took off in a dash.
Ramone stood, awaiting
A green flag to flash.

Time gone on the clock,
The race now was done.
His friends were in shock.
Ramone had not won.

Concerned, they looked on,
Then ran up to him.
"Ramone, what is wrong?
Why didn't you win?"

"Well, I've kept a secret.
I beg you, be kind.
My vision's imperfect.
See, I'm color blind."

"Ramone, we're your mates
And we love you no less.
We'll help you be great
With your color-blindness."

Ramone slowly brightened
He thought, "Oh, I know
I need flags with writing:
One STOP and one GO."

His pals took the pace
And wrote words on the flags.
Now all horses could race,
Even short-sighted nags.

Ramone was relieved.
His friends had been sweet.
There had never been need
For his secret to keep.

8. Elton

Oh, those pigs in the sty
With a gleam in their eye,
Roll in the muck
And with any luck

Lie in filth, filth, filth,
Filled with tilth, tilth, tilth.

They roll and they smile.
Oh, the pigs all the while,
Love the smell and the stench
Where they live in the trench

Of the grime, grime, grime,
All the time, time, time

But not Elton!

Elton likes surroundings neat.
When you visit, wipe your feet,
And politely sit on benches,
Keeping tidy all the trenches.

At his home, home, home,
All alone, lone, lone.

Elton keeps himself so clean,
Prepares delicious French cuisine.
The other pigs all found him weird
And never, ever, ever neared

Elton's pen, pen, pen,
In the glen, glen, glen.

But then one day the pigs grew bored
Of stench and grime of sweaty horde.
Instead, they wanted to be dry.
So they all went to Elton's sty.

With a grin, grin, grin,
They went in, in, in.

Elton welcomed all the pigs
To his super-tidy digs,
Made them wash before they dined,
Got them really quite refined.

With some style, style, style,
They did smile, smile, smile.

Finest manners they did use
When he served them apple juice.
Napkins tucked beneath their snouts
While they ate their brussel sprouts.

Keeping clean, clean, clean,
Like a queen, queen, queen.

Elton, left with muddy floors,
Fin'ly closed the barnyard doors.
But he really didn't mind
Since the pigs had been so kind.

He has friends, friends, friends
In his pen, pen, pen.

9. Riddhi

Riddhi here, Riddhi there,
Hopping, hopping everywhere.

Jumping up, jumping down,
Swiftest bunny in this town.

Looking left, looking right—
Are there enemies in sight?
Tail goes up, fluff of white,
Nose is twitching fast as light.

Gotta move, can't sit still,
Running up the bunny hill.
Moving fast, just one goal:
Diving down the rabbit hole.

Safely in my cozy den
Heart beats fast like wings of wren.
Nerves a wreck, must get calm,
Cup of tea might be the balm.

Breathing deep like I've been taught.
Meditate on peaceful thoughts.
Douse the lamp, rest my eyes
A calmer rabbit now inside.

10. Malarkey Mouse

Malarkey Mouse
Could eat a house
If time were on his side.

A nibble here,
A gobble there,
He liked to eat things fried.

He thought of food
In every mood
And constantly was chewing.

On candies, cakes,
On bread and bakes—
'Til food was his undoing.

His giant frame
Was all to blame:
He couldn't leave his house.

His knees would hurt,
Sink to the dirt.
There's one unhappy mouse.

One day his brother
And his mother
Sought to get him moving.

They made for him
An in-house gym.
His weight began improving.

He walked each day
And stayed away
From sugared snacks and treats.

Ate salads, fruit,
And cheese to boot.
He finally saw his feet.

Now mouse felt great!
He'd lost the weight
And walked out that front door.

Healthy and fit,
Proud every bit.
And cuter than before!

11. Latisha Llama

Latisha Llama wants her mama.
When Mom's not home it's quite the drama.

Wailing, shouting, all day pouting…
For Mama Llama there's no outing.

Latisha Llama fears that Mama
Will go outdoors and have a trauma.

Though Mama knows it's no big deal,
Latisha thinks it's all too real.

Then Mama Llama has a thought
So Latisha will not be distraught.

Perhaps she'd like some kind of pet.
When Mom goes out, she will not fret.

A kitten just might do the trick—
A fuzzy ball of fur named Mick.

When Mick came home, Latisha thrilled.
The kitten's love kept her fulfilled.

To test things, Mom went to the store.
Wet-eyed, Latisha closed the door.

Mick mewed a bit. He wanted food.
Latisha giggled as he chewed.

Before she knew it, Mom was back.
Latisha's mood was right on track.

"I missed you, Mom, and cried a bit,
But Mick was here to help with it."

"I love you, girl, I always do.
But sometimes I can't be with you.

So don't be sad. You're not alone
You've love to give until I'm home."

12. Dudley the Donkey

Dudley the donkey is full of tall tales.
He's visited kings and he's swum with whales
He's met Elvis Presley; he's sung at the Met.
He's fluent in French and in Spanish, you bet.

To Dudley the donkey his own life is boring
So he makes up lies to keep others from snoring.
He wants to be noticed within his herd,
But no one believes a single word.

One day he wanted to tell them a truth.
That hadn't happened since Dudley's youth.
"There's a winter storm coming as big as can be.
We need to prepare or we'll freeze here, you see?"

The herd of donkeys said, "Sure, yeah, right.
What else are you gonna tell us tonight?
You never tell the truth anyhow
So why should we all believe you now?"

The herd turned their backs, and away they went,
Skipping in donkey merriment.
Poor Dudley, he knew that he'd been wrong
To tell such lies to them all along.

This time he needed all their trust.
Instead they left him in disgust.
Panicked, he grabbed a radio
And blared the news about the snow.

Startled, the donkeys turned around.
Shock on their faces could be found.
"Never again," Dudley said in a roar.
"I will not lie to you anymore."

Dudley found blankets in the barn.
The family of donkeys hunkered down.
Inside they snuggled, nice and warm
Dudley the donkey was now reformed.

Peacefully, The End.

AcuteByDesign
the little book company that could
A Michael Marion Sharpe Company

Some other AcuteByDesign books you may enjoy:

There's a Tiger in My House
by Michael Marion Sharpe,
Illustrated by Chris Burton

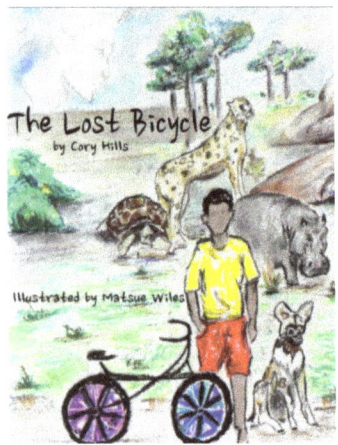

The Lost Bicycle
By Cory Hills,
Illustrated by Matsue Wiles

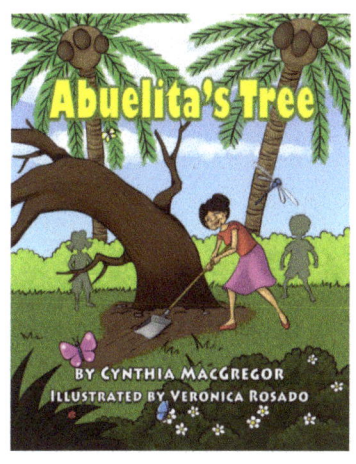

Abuelita's Tree

By Cynthia MacGregor,
Illustrated by Veronica Rosado

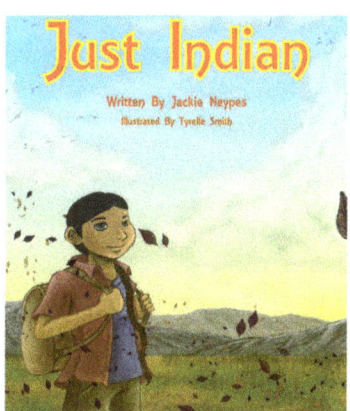

Just Indian

By Jackie Neypes,
Illustrated by Tyrelle Smith

This is just a sampling of our wonderful multicultural offerings. Please visit www.AcuteByDesign.com to see our full line of books.

AcuteByDesign
the little book company that could
A Michael Marion Sharpe Company

www.ingramcontent.com/pod-product-compliance
Lightning Source LLC
Chambersburg PA
CBHW041220240426

43661CB00012B/1098